Left-Handed Wolf

LEFT-HANDED

LOUISIANA STATE UNIVERSITY PRESS / BATON ROUGE

POEMS

WOLF

ADAM DAY

Published by Louisiana State University Press
Manufactured in the United States of America
LSU Press Paperback Original
First printing

DESIGNER: Michelle A. Neustrom
TYPEFACE: Sina Nova
PRINTER AND BINDER: LSI

Many thanks to the editors of the following journals, where versions of some of
these poems first appeared: *Bad Nudes, Boston Review, Diagram, Gasher, The Hollins
Critic, Mascara Literary Review* (Australia), *The Maynard* (Canada), *Nightblock, North
American Review, Posit, Sou'Wester, Sequstrum, Sidereal Magazine, Sow's Ear, The
Spectacle, Thrush, Tusculum Review, Takahē* (New Zealand), *Witness,* and *Whiskey
Island.* Special thanks to MaryKatherine Callaway, Alisa Plant, James Long, Neal
Novak, and everyone else at LSU Press who made this book possible.

LIBRARY OF CONGRESS CATALOGING-IN-PUBLICATION DATA
Names: Day, Adam, 1977– author.
Title: Left-handed wolf : poems / Adam Day.
Description: Baton Rouge : Louisiana State University Press, 2020.
Identifiers: LCCN 2019036614 (print) | LCCN 2019036615 (ebook) | ISBN 978-0-8071-
    7107-3 (paperback) | ISBN 978-0-8071-7326-8 (pdf) | ISBN 978-0-8071-7327-5 (epub)
Subjects: LCGFT: Poetry.
Classification: LCC PS3604.A9798 L44 2020 (print) | LCC PS3604.A9798 (ebook) |
    DDC 811/.6—dc23
LC record available at https://lccn.loc.gov/2019036614
LC ebook record available at https://lccn.loc.gov/2019036615

If you meet the Buddha on the road, kill him.

—LINJI YIXUAN

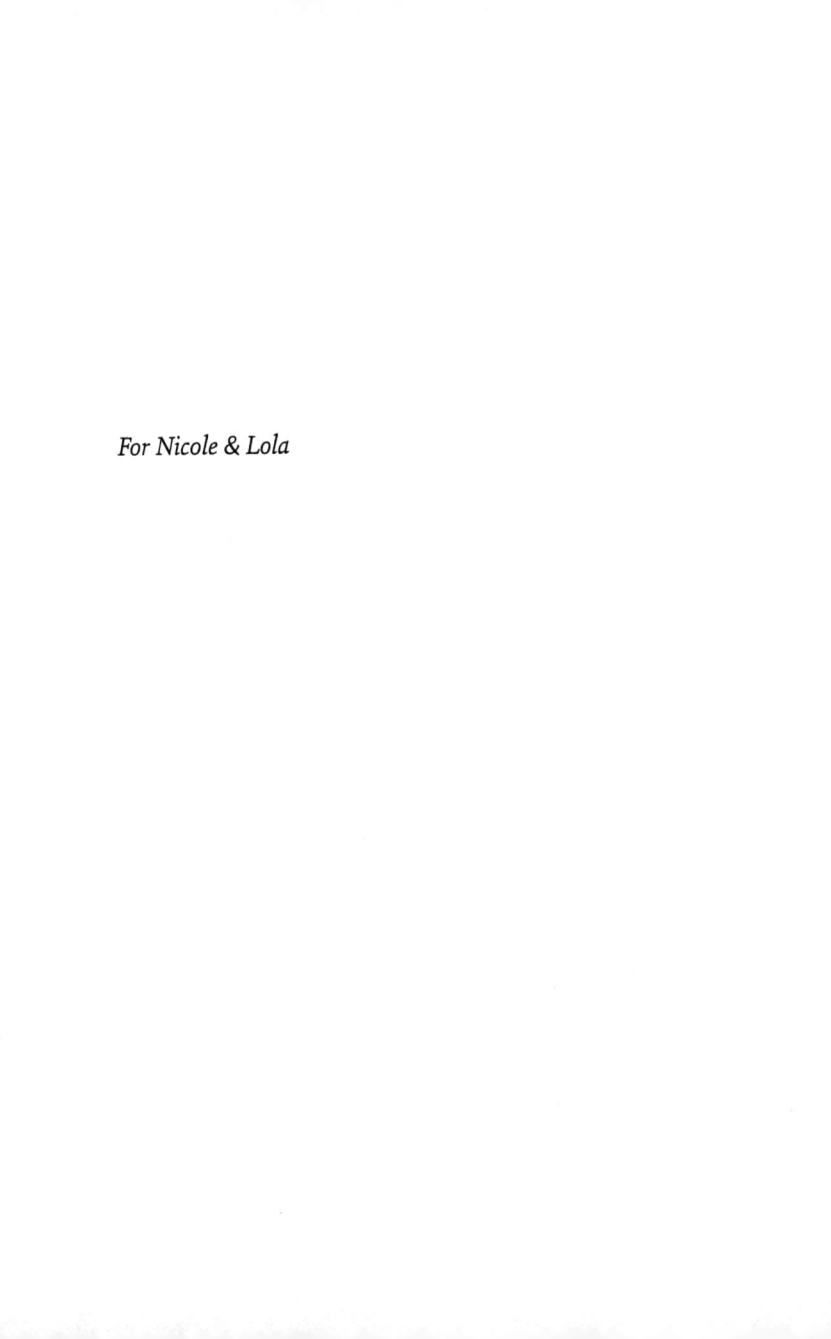

For Nicole & Lola

CONTENTS

The titles of these poems are derived, in part, from language associated with the various strains of Buddhism and Buddhist meditation. A lack of familiarity with any of the terms will do nothing to diminish the reader's experience, and there is no need to distract from the reading experience by looking up the terms.

Numbers or symbols were considered, but they seemed *too* anonymous. In a sense, the current titles are meaningful placeholders, much the way the breath is. We don't assign a meaning to the breath, per se, but the space it might create, what it might perhaps deliver us from or to, is of substance. The poems themselves are what are urgent here, I hope.

Left-Handed Wolf

Guanyin

It rained
so neighbor

walked barefoot
through brightwork

of parked
and rolling cars,

sewn inside
his coat. Best place

to hide something
is in

the present; no one
looks there.

Chakgya

Sex in public,
eyeing the mountains

behind the mountains,
like boy Scouts

rubbing sticks
together in the dark.

Jhana

Streetlight reflected
in raindrops shaken

from a crane's bill.
Caught between, caught

without.

Pattini

The tree is smarter, it
has stopped moving.

Saba

Silence amid swinging birdfeeders,
the moon dragging its tail

behind silver pines, cold
in falling night. It drops

into the green river, glowing
ditch-dog, and the water is cool.

The chilled crane in its cloud
nest hasn't roused yet. Lives

in between. Smug motherfucker.

Pella

Two men in the woods, young
in shirts and shoes, hair

in hands. Tall grass,
wet calves. Reeds

at the red legs
of electrical towers,

pimpled with bolt-heads.

Satori

Ripple of wrists
disappearing

around cove rock
beneath ferns

and shadow
of low-skimming

tern.

Bosatsu Basswood

A negotiation of desire
touched more by imbalance

than grace, like the birdhouse-
shitting sparrow.

Chenrezig

Scarlet and cobalt
paper lanterns

hung with icicles.
The caribou all call

together. Smoking
muzzles,

blue mouths
in January.

Yuugen Gulf

Fog sheet from cloud
to ground. Mahogany water
of the mare's dead eye.

Eko

All the cupboards
thrown open; interloping

blue-winged teal
in a tub of dirty bathwater.

Night sky muzzling the moon—clouds
and contrails. Dead martins

tossed into the flooded
culvert, like standing beside

a lice comb at the edge of space;
they know something I don't.

Gompa

The aspen is not
a tree. Cliff martin

has the moon
in its throat. Flood

rain banked
in the channel ditch;

red spores of mud water.
Plumes of exhaust

torn away
in brake light.

Gyana

Midnight rain
windows. Threads

of thunder
in street runoff.

Slobber-lipped
sailor feeding money

to the cigarette machine.

Samatha

Nuthatch
in the gutter;

cut-throat cock
on the table

with a bowl
for its blood

and a pile of leeks.

Abhinaya

Ignorant birds
sank the cadavers

in dusk straits
of the between.

Leaf-footed
bug on an eyelid

like snow
on an asshole.

Ordinarily we
look away.

Rechungpa

Blue spruce steam
above stone houses.

And no one
knows. Or sees

a water tower begin
to walk into

a green bay. The locks
yawn loose. Sky

draws a white sheet
over the island's

neighborhood of tame
houses, and a pulsing, blue-rippled light

in coastal darkness, like something
that has a choice.

Swati

Weedy copse,
frost apples

on the trees. She lay
for three days,

one side
of her face

in mud before
they scrape

beneath her nails.
Thing without

thinking. Palms
like smeared newspaper,

blackened fingertips. Masked
cardinal burning

on a branch.

Vayāna

Beyond the dunes, pairs
of gunmetal giant ibis,

bits of string
in nervous beaks. Wind blows

tarps off tanks,
secreted on the beach, like children

with their mania
for taking out

dolls' eyes to see
what's behind. Cumbersome

empire.

Bhogakaya

Kids jumping off ruined
jetty ends

into the sea. They swarm
ruins, veil the world

that was. Music echoes
from a flood-control chamber.

A couch is lifted
to the light. Night abandoned

sewer, raining outside
phosphorous flares, barrel

bombs. A few candles
in here; some loiter near

the entrance, watch
flames light

and fade, chatter,
nudge, point. Strange generation.

Jamyang

At night, the babies
are passed down

the cots, suckling
useless tits

of men. They favored
the fattest among us.

We could hear
soldiers coming

from some desert
of frost, eating

their own light, driving
flocks of oryx

before them.

Godo

This was not
the world. I was told

that these
are human

beings—they did not
look like

human beings.

Jokai

Hawk owls
and calandras

fly into clouds
for good. Lines

that devour
their own nature.

Fudo In

Stars break chairs
and the plants

smell red
in the night.

Densu Swale

Eyes at sea, he ducks
in and out of traffic, throws

dud punches
that should've landed

last deployment. So, men
show him how to eat

his own mouth, the clumsy
hot lowing throat gulps

and leave him
overnight to linger like a mote

of light in buffalo grass,
plum bushes; a vein

of blood skating
the blue plate

of his good eye.

Alder Svara

Moonlight pales
limbs. Closed eyes

less distracted. Green
wind, thin leaves. Breath

and body, waves
and sea. Corncrakes

talk in the shallows
and supplejack.

Paramita

Hard the black bear
has to work

to speak, accosting
the boulder

for its lack
of ambition, its absence

of anger,
its need

for touch.

Rigpa

Grey heron
in the snowfield

hides in its figure,
opening the letter

that never arrived.
In the blueness

of the hour
when I stretch

my spine
the trees

are taking
off their leaves

and I am
out of context.

Kosha

Mud-footed lilies
below pylons strung

with sagging electrical cables,
silver oak disinterred

from a bog. Stone wall
in early snow.

Samadhi

Day is late and has
no horse. Icicles

on concertina wire. Blue ridges
blackening. Buoy bells

in fog; groaning
pylons. Boat hidden

in cape reeds. A body
neatly disposed of

floating to the surface. Plank
in reason. Doesn't fuck with

what comes up.

Juzu Shade

Sick of fixing the car
and of red trees in autumn

hills. Grasshoppers
crackle on concrete. Waiting

for something
to happen. Still

shit water
mirrors clear light.

Ash Arhat

Crumbling headstones
used to grind tea. Grass

does bend to the sea. Still,
he's afraid

of not being
anymore. Others exist.

He must.

Kapala

The little girls from down the road
don't take shit. Hate witnesses.

They're up the red oaks. Cigarette
filters crushed in ironweed. Bone

and amaranth clouds piss into the river
horizon. Screen door smacks in wind.

Yard of broken bricks; two dead moles
blue in the dusk. Walking out finally

across the damp grass, drunk,
toward the river.

Shinkin

Drinking
her own milk

like a sailor
singing into

a rock wall.
Can't see the hand

but its shadow.

Dianthus Chidar

Damp darkness. Moths
in black grass. Exhausted

morning, colorless
lake. The body below

looks more and more
like the earth next to it.

Public works plug
eye sockets with sod.

Collar bones
mounted on a wall,

most kings get their heads
cut off.

Niguma

Undrowned but often
almost drowning, she

has chosen the baby
to include as herself, leaves

behind the bearer of axle grease
knuckles. Motor pants

like a forest
of bandage-eyed owls. Strange

how differently
joy operates these days. Still,

she doesn't know
what's beyond that stand of trees

or what's keeping it. Hard to convey
the space she is when she steps

finally off the subway, whipped
air at the swaddled's head. There are

several thousand ways to kill a man.

Anju

Distant skyscrapers,
half-lit. Sparks spread

under the subway shrugged
from tunnel night. Wolf moves

unevenly over flat earth, panting
at the effort. Inside,

I'm writing more shit
about new snow.

Jātaka Thangka

In the place where everyone
forgets that they

have forgotten, she shouts
at the greyhounds, 'Come on,

you one-eared bastard.' Just this
is it. Blue ridges blackening

out back, while a puzzled bus
lurches to a stop like the past

one wants back.

Nikāya

A thing
in me
a bird
or something
smashing snails
open, dragging
dark waters.

Purana

Wind lifts snow
from beach. Foam

frozen in scalloped
edges. Black water

slashed white.
Shearwater

strangles on a length
of fishline. Witness

to its own humiliation.

Muted Janpe

Boats step
through ice, geese

barking and dark
water under a shelf

of snow. Saturn's rings
become the cast-iron

balcony of a house
seen from everywhere.

Sukha

Snow makes
the mountain. White

streets, blue shudders.
Spooked hare

moves ass
over ice-pasture.

Inji Moss

For the Rohingya

Killdeer cut tweescreams
across slate

sky. There are teak trees
with their heads

blown off. No monks
on the green and cream

mountains. Just the corpulent
branches of banyans

low hung above the dying
that langurs clamber

over. And goddamn
truth always changing.

Osho

Homing bells ring
in mountain fog,

where lynx
have been. Sleeves

wet, mind
on beetling around

abandoned housing projects—ceiling rain
from waylaid pipes,

streaming stairwells—
where my cousins lived.

Set for demolition.
Vacant rooms

of dust
and animal tracks.

Jamgon Thaye

Ghost aren't the dead;
they're black ox

bending tall grass
horns plowing

clouds, lightning
silence, spray of earth

thrown off the split seams
of strip mines, lightly

blue-veined skin
at tops of breasts, brawling

sparrows building
human ears of nests,

inscribed into past
and change, the tac-

ti-tac of a train
striking the hours off.

Winkaya

Bird-shit-bleached house has gone
back to snow. Mockingbird

up on a line, fucking
with the noise ordinance.

Maitri Upacara

Pulled weeds, stray cat
in the rabbit trap. Plants

grow between bricks. Vehicle
of some kind.

Gandharan

She stands on lichen-coated
bricks, barefoot with stashed

eyes. All are inside,
awake, in their rooms,

politely not a-swarm
and slightly missed. Shored

against ruin. Still
storm petrels move

in birch tops. Smacking
of sea water on either side of her.

Mantak

Nine flies
on the bathroom

window. A kind of map
of white America,

spectral and supernatural,
the silent salesman,

a triangulation of desire.

Sakra

Pinned to the lawn
with croquet wickets. If he existed

she'd divorce him. Tree is gone
but the shadow stands.

Yidam

Words are not quite words
so we can talk. Seeing

sometimes the hundred
grass tips, ice shelf

rift and calve. Land
that never has been yet.

The bobcat at least
has the sense to eat

its afterbirth.

Parikamma

Wake early just to sit
on my ass. Split

whale wrecked in primer gray
rain waves

at the blunt cape head.
The ocean

a heap of water, the eye
a sea.

Yamantaka

Spotted deer wonder
down shore to graze

on seaweed. Below
a passing prow,

some body tills
the sea floor

in blue flame.
Awkward stars;

sluggish wave-growl.

Abhaya

Kites steal entrails
boat-tossed by an angler.

Squatting macaques
yawn on shore,

smacking clams open
on stones.

Feldspar Citta

Pinyon jay stalks a stone
the color of fat,

on moist turf. Circling, tries
to get in with its beak

but there is nothing
to get into. More tired.

Honzan

Island in the middle
of everywhere. One skua

with a wing dragging
like a banner

humps down shore. Who
ever deserves

anything anyway?
A stupid concept.

Chinmaya

The man wakes up
hard on the north shore

of the river
where willow roots

vein the ground. Bats rock
in the furrows

of the water face. Those aren't
quite hands they have.

Amida

Bathing now, eyes
drawn to the wide-wrinkled

two-potato sack of balls
at his crotch

like soldiers on tour
staring at strange ground.

Ganapati Brume

Out past the skeletons
of car plants and the eyes

of iced ponds, past
canal machinery

and green shadows
of bulk-bins, the liquid

echo of nightjars.

Lambent Prana

Blueweed sky
beneath archipelago

of cypress tops, making space
for silence.

Nagarjun

Cornflower skink
walks the evening

wall, from nowhere,
to nowhere.

Guhyasamaja

Hunger watching out
from the stars

and black fields
of cold bodies,

the eyes and hidden
mouths of stone

and light, saying only
come closer.

Koji

Even on the central mountain
there is melt. River snow

in a field of thunder; sirius falls
apart. No goddamn rainbow

mists or women
like irises.

Dosan

Streamside trees, auburn
in what is left of spring.

Ripe persimmons cling
to a flint wall. A sluggish

truck makes its way
up the hillside. The factories

aren't coming back. The headless bull
wanders into the bog; it's not

the moon, but awake.

Hanami

Blue mountain
makes white
clouds. The trees
are pulling up
anchor.

NOTES

This book owes a debt to the life and work of
Michael Stone.

The following also played a very real role in the creation
of these poems: Jean-Michel Basquiat; Kobayashi Issa;
Jeff Mueller of the band June of 44; Carlos Oquendo
deGandharan; Darcie Dennigan; Maurice Merleau-Ponty
and Walter Benjamin; Dōgen; Jan Karski; Ikkyū; Katie
Alice Greer of the band Priests; John Ashbery's "The
Skaters"; Emily Dickinson's "I Felt a Funeral, in my Brain";
Frank O'Hara's poems "Stag Club," "F.Y.I. (Prix de Beauté)"
and "Returning"; Thomas Pynchon's novel *V.;* and David
Alworth's *Site Reading: Fiction, Art, Social Form.*

CPSIA information can be obtained
at www.ICGtesting.com
Printed in the USA
LVHW021950180220
647337LV00007B/925

9 780807 171073